Crystal

From

Mom (Phylis)

Date

Dec. 11, 2012

Little Messengers of Comfort

Artwork by

Carolyn Shores Wright

HARVEST HOUSE PUBLISHERS

EUGENE, OREGON

Little Messengers of Comfort

Copyright © 2009 by Harvest House Publishers
Published by Harvest House Publishers
Eugene, Oregon 97402
www.harvesthousepublishers.com

ISBN 978-0-7369-2481-8

Artwork designs are reproduced under license from Carolyn Shores Wright/© C. Shores, Inc. Courtesy of Artworks! Licensing LLC and may not be reproduced without permission. For more information regarding art prints in this book, please contact:

> Artworks! Licensing
> 10099 SE White Pelican Way
> Jupiter, FL 33469
> 561-745-6484

Design and production by Garborg Design Works, Savage, Minnesota

Printed in China

11 12 13 14 15 / LP / 10 9 8 7 6 5 4 3

Words of comfort,
skillfully administered,
are the oldest therapy
known to man.

LOUIS NIZER

Ah, Hope! What would life be,
stripped of thy encouraging smiles,
that teach us to look behind the
dark clouds of today, for the golden
beams that are to gild the morrow.

SUSANNA MOODIE

In the midst of winter,
I found there was, within me,
an invincible summer.

ALBERT CAMUS

When the heart is enlivened again, it feels like the sun coming out after a week of rainy days. There is hope in the heart that chases the clouds away. Hope is a higher heart frequency, and as you begin to reconnect with your heart, hope is waiting to show you new possibilities and arrest the downward spiral of grief and loneliness. It becomes a matter of how soon you want the sun to shine. Listening to the still, small voice in your heart will make hope into a reality.

SARA PADDISON

There is nothing better than th

ncouragement of a good friend.

KATHARINE BUTLER HATHAWAY

Great is my confidence in
you, great is my boasting
on your behalf; I am
filled with comfort.

THE BOOK of 2 CORINTHIANS

Lord, lift my eyes above the circumstances of the moment so I can see the purpose for which You created me. Help me to clearly hear Your call on my life and realize who I am in Christ.

STORMIE OMARTIAN

When praying for healing, ask great things of God and expect great things from God.

ARLO F. NEWELL

*I will heal
them and
reveal to them
the abundance
of peace
and truth.*

THE BOOK OF JEREMIAH

*Learn from yesterday, live for today,
hope for tomorrow.*

AUTHOR UNKNOWN

The past is a guidepost, not a hitching post.

L. Thomas Holdcroft

Treasure the memories that comfort you,
and explore those that may trouble you.
Even difficult memories can help us to
heal. Share memories with those who
listen well and support you. Recognize
that your memories may make you laugh
or cry. It's important to remember that
healing doesn't mean forgetting.

Author Unknown

Faith, like

Be strong and of good courage; do not be afraid, nor dismayed, for the LORD your God is with you wherever you go.

THE BOOK OF JOSHUA

muscle, grows by stretching.

A.W. TOZER

When the divine owner takes possession of a property, he has a twofold objective: intense cultivation and abounding fruitfulness.

NORMAN P. GRUBB

Accept life daily not as a cup to be drained but as a chalice to be filled with whatsoever things are honest, pure, lovely, and of good report.

Sydney Lovett

Every problem is just a

...opportunity waiting to be made use of.

Some of the things we lift up in prayer are difficult and frightening. But He promises to always be with us.

ELIZABETH GEORGE

Hope and fear are inseparable.

LA ROCHEFOUCAULD

Cast your bread upon the waters, for after many days you will find it again.

THE BOOK OF ECCLESIASTES

I am a most noteworthy sinner, but I have cried out to the Lord for grace and mercy, and they have covered me completely. I have found the sweetest consolation since I made it my whole purpose to enjoy His marvellous Presence.

CHRISTOPHER COLUMBUS

*May he give you
the desire of your
heart and make all
your plans succeed.*

THE BOOK OF PSALMS

*Life is not meant to
be easy, my child;
but take courage—
it can be delightful.*

GEORGE BERNARD SHAW

A willing heart adds feather to the heel.

JOANNA BAILLIE

No matter how late the hour, no matter how desperate the moment, we cannot despair; the joy and riches God has promised us stretch like a shining road into the future!

CATHERINE MARSHALL

Be joyful in hope, patient in affliction

$\mathcal{L}$ord, I pray for Your healing touch on my life. Please make every part of my body function as it is designed to, and wherever there is anything out of balance, set it in perfect working order. Help me remember that there is a time for healing, and even when I pray and don't have immediate results, I can always trust You, my Maker.

STORMIE OMARTIAN

faithful in prayer.

THE BOOK OF ROMANS

In thy word, Lord, is my trust
To thy mercies fast I fly;
Though I am but clay and dust,
Yet thy grace can lift me high.

THOMAS CAMPION
"A Prayer for Grace"

O beloved, I plead with you not to
treat God's promises as something
to be displayed in a museum but
to use them as everyday sources of
comfort. And whenever you have a
time of need, trust the Lord.

CHARLES H. SPURGEON

*I*n order to capture the present, we need to give less attention to worries, mistakes, what's going wrong, general concerns, things to get done, the past, the future, and the undone. Today I will only think about today. No regrets for the past or fears about the future. When you do this, all your focus is on the now. You can smile, laugh, pray, think, and enjoy what each moment brings.

EMILIE BARNES

Behind all this, some grea

happiness is hiding.

YEHUDA AMICHAI

Only those who dare to fai

Most of the important things in the
world have been accomplished by
people who have kept on trying when
there seemed to be no hope at all.

DALE CARNEGIE

greatly can ever achieve greatly.

ROBERT F. KENNEDY

*Delight yourself in the LORD and he
will give you the desires of your heart.*

THE BOOK OF PSALMS

Piglet had got up early that morning to pick himself a bunch of violets; and when he had picked them and put them in a pot in the middle of his house, it suddenly came over him that nobody had ever picked Eeyore a bunch of violets, and the more he thought of this, the more he thought how sad it was to be an Animal who had never had a bunch of violets picked for him. So he hurried out again, saying to himself, "Eeyore, Violets," and then "Violets, Eeyore," in case he forgot, because it was that sort of day.

A.A. MILNE
The House at Pooh Corner

I know Christ dwells within me all the time, guiding me and inspiring me whenever I do or say anything. A light of which I caught no glimmer before comes to me at the very moment when it is needed.

SAINT THÉRÈSE OF LISIEUX

May the God of hope fill you with all joy and peace as you trust in him, so that you may overflow with hope by the power of the Holy Spirit.

THE BOOK OF ROMANS

If a care is too small to be turned into a prayer, it is too small to be made into a burden.

CORRIE TEN BOOM

Those who are willing to be vulnerable move among mysteries.

THEODORE ROETHKE

Take time to be holy,
Be calm in thy soul,
Each tho't and each motive
Beneath His control.

WILLIAM D. LONGSTAFF
"Take Time to Be Holy"

$\mathcal{S}$he could not speak, but she did "hold on," and the warm grasp of the friendly human hand comforted her sore heart, and seemed to lead her nearer to the Divine arm which alone could uphold her in her trouble.

LOUISA MAY ALCOTT

May your unfailing love be my comfort,
according to your promise to your servant.
Let your compassion come to me that I
may live, for your law is my delight.

THE BOOK OF PSALMS

The timid and fearful first failures dismay,
But the stout heart stays trying by night and by day.
He values his failures as lessons that teach
The one way to get to the goal he would reach.

EDGAR A. GUEST

Our greatest glory is not in never falling

Character cannot be developed in ease and quiet.
Only through experiences of trial and suffering
can the soul be strengthened, vision cleared,
ambition inspired, and success achieved.

HELEN KELLER

…ut in rising every time we fall.

OLIVER GOLDSMITH

*Other refuge have I none; hangs my
helpless soul on Thee;
Leave, ah! leave me not alone, still
support and comfort me.
All my trust on Thee is stayed, all
my help from Thee I bring;
Cover my defenseless head with the
shadow of Thy wing.*

CHARLES WESLEY
"Jesus, Lover of My Soul"

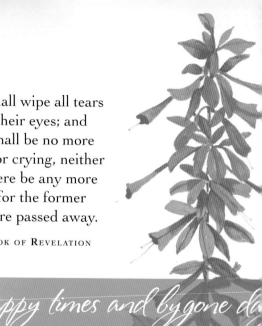

$\mathcal{G}$od shall wipe all tears
from their eyes; and
there shall be no more
death, nor crying, neither
shall there be any more
pain: for the former
things are passed away.

THE BOOK OF REVELATION

Happy times and bygone da

they grow more wonderful with

are never lost...In truth,
the heart that keeps them.

KAY ANDREW

A cloudy day is no match

When comforts are declining,
He grants the soul again
A season of clear shining,
To cheer it after rain.

WILLIAM COWPER

*We may run, walk, stumble, drive,
or fly, but let us never lose sight of
the reason for the journey or miss a
chance to see a rainbow on the way.*

GLORIA GAITHER

for a sunny disposition.

WILLIAM ARTHUR WARD

*C*omfort—a simple seven-letter word. It's a word with numerous meanings. It can mean strengthening aid, consolation in time of trouble or worry, a feeling of relief or encouragement, or easing the grief or trouble of. Is this your situation? Is it relief that you need right now? Is there some way in which you need to be encouraged? What is the grief in your life that you would like to see lifted at this time? Right now, your desire is probably for the companionship of comfort. Perhaps you're one of those who wonders if there is any comfort to be had…

Comfort will come and perhaps when and where you least expect it. Hold on to this knowledge—it may take your head to convince your heart that it is so. Your grief will *not* last forever. It may seem that way, but eventually it will subside.

H. Norman Wright

Grief knits two hearts in closer bonds than happiness ever can; and common sufferings are far stronger links than common joys.

ALPHONSE DE LAMARTINE

The friend who can be silent with us in a moment of despair or confusion, who can stay with us in an hour of grief and bereavement, who can tolerate not knowing...not healing, not curing...that is a friend who cares.

HENRI NOUWEN

We must accept finite disappointment, but we must never lose infinite hope.

MARTIN LUTHER KING

Our life is like a tapestry of intricate design
With lovely patterns taking shape as colors
intertwine,
Some of the threads we weave ourselves
By things we choose to do—
Sometimes a loving Father's touch
adds a special hue.
And though tomorrow's pattern is not
for us to see—
We can trust his faithful hand through
all eternity.

AUTHOR UNKNOWN

Just as despair can come to one only from other human beings, hope, too, can be given to one only by other human beings.

ELIE WEISEL

*L*ife is made up, not of great sacrifices or duties, but of little things, in which smiles and kindness, and small obligations given habitually, are what preserve the heart and secure comfort.

HUMPHRY DAVY

*L*ord, I know I can trust You in the midst of a trial, because You measure the weight of it on my shoulders. You alone are my refuge and my strength. I come to Your throne and ask for grace and patience as I seek You for help in this time of need.

STORMIE OMARTIAN

Courage is like love; it must

Be strong and courageous…for
the LORD your God…will never
leave you nor forsake you.

THE BOOK OF DEUTERONOMY

Nothing is so strong as
gentleness and nothing is
so gentle as real strength.

RALPH W. SOCKMAN

have hope for nourishment.

Napoleon I

We find comfort among those who agr

Along the Road

I walked a mile with Pleasure;
She chattered all the way.
But left me none the wiser
For all she had to say.
I walked a mile with Sorrow
And ne'er a word said she;
But oh, the things I learned from her
When Sorrow walked with me!

ROBERT BROWNING

ith us—growth among those who don't.

FRANK A. CLARK

God writes with a pen that never blots,
speaks with a tongue that never slips, and
acts with a hand that never fails.

AUTHOR UNKNOWN

Headlong joy is ever on the wing.

JOHN MILTON

It is from books that wise people derive
consolation in the troubles of life.

VICTOR HUGO

Hope, the best comfort of our imperfect condition.

EDWARD GIBBON